Advance Praise for *Do More*

"I've had more than my share of tragic loss over the years, including my beloved brother, Offir, and my father. I was filled with tears of both sadness and joy when I read Brad Capurro's wonderful and bittersweet work, *Do More.* I can't tell you how many people I have come across who regret that they didn't demonstrate more love and affection to those they hold dear while they had the chance. This endearing book is filled with inspiring poetry, photographs, reminiscences, and gentle nudges that will make you think and feel more deeply about your own life and, ultimately, make you smile."

—**Tsikki Thau**, internationally acclaimed stress management expert and manifestation coach and author of *Attract It All: The Real Secret to Manifestatio*

"Deeply emotional, raw, and beautifully vulnerable. *Do More* inspires us to simply love with intention, reminding us of life's fragility. Grief demands we Do More now."

—**Mary Ann Ricciardi**, author of
Screaming Through the Silence

"*Do Mor*e gently and thoughtfully reminds us that death comes for all, including those loved ones we hope to be with us always. Even more importantly the book kindly urges us to "do more" to manifest our love. There are few more urgent messages for our times."

—**Donald E. Hardy**, professor emeritus,
University of Nevada, Reno

DO MORE

How to Fully Love and Celebrate Your Special People While They Are Still Here

BRAD CAPURRO

GMK WRITING AND EDITING, INC.

Published by GMK Writing and Editing, Inc.

Produced by GMK Writing and Editing, Inc.
Managing Editor: Katie Benoit
Copyedited by Ilana Krebs
Proofread by Amy Gordon
Composition by Libby Kingsbury
Cover and interior design by Vicky Vaughn Shea
Printed by IngramSpark

Interior and front cover illustrations by Bob Koehler

All prose and poetry by the author

Print ISBN: 978-1-966981-22-0
Ebook EISN: 978-1-966981-23-7

Visit the author at DoMoreOften.com

This work was written, designed, and produced without the use of AI (Artificial Intelligence). Human creativity and intelligence may not be perfect, but they are far better than anything artificial.

Note: This publication is presented solely for informational, educational, and entertainment purposes. It is not intended to provide personal, relationship, legal, financial, or other advice and should not be relied upon as such. If expert assistance is required, the services of a professional should be sought. The publisher and the author and their affiliated entities and individuals do not make any guarantees or other promises as to any results that may be obtained from using the content of this book. To the maximum extent permitted by law, the publisher and the author and their affiliated entities and individuals disclaim any and all liability in the event any information contained in this book proves to be inaccurate, incomplete, or unreliable, or results any harm or loss. You, the reader, are responsible for your own choices, actions, and results.

This book is dedicated, with love, to Rachel, Brittany, Tony, Teagan, Remi, Cruz, and Cash. My wish for each of you is that throughout your life, you will always strive to Do More than Just Stay.

Acknowledgments

Sending love and appreciation to all my wonderful friends and family members who have heard me, held me, and loved me over the entirety of my life and, most importantly, on my darkest days.

A special thanks to those who assisted me throughout the creation of *Do More* by selflessly giving your time, talents, emotional support, and love. I hope that you know who you are and how much I treasure the time we shared during this beautiful journey.

My heartfelt thanks to the following individuals: Don Hardy, for your insight and encouragement. Bob Koehler, for your kind and caring manner as you crafted the beautiful illustrations included in these pages. Gary Krebs, Katie Benoit, Ilana Krebs, Libby Kingsbury, Amy Gordon, and Vicky Shea, for your skillful production of *Do More* and your welcoming, personal approach to the book production process.

Preface

Whether we know it's coming, or it crashes in without warning, grief shakes everything it touches. It changes everything we think we know—about life, about love, about ourselves. As a grief therapist, I have spent hundreds, maybe thousands of hours sitting with people in their pain—helping them name it, helping them feel it, helping them find a way to carry it forward. Personally, I have carried grief with me like a shadow for most of my life. It has been a heavy, yet quiet companion for many years. It has broken me, shaken me, and shaped me. Though brutal at times, it laid the path for me to have the honor of walking so many others through their own grief journeys—a job I wouldn't trade for the world. And yet, nothing could have prepared me for the pain that came from losing my mother—nor for the lonely, hollow quiet that would follow in her absence. When my mother died, the world shifted in a way that words will never be able to capture.

My father has always been a man of integrity—a man who values honesty, even when faced with pressure to concede—to do the easier, expected thing. This book is a beautiful example of his refusal to go along with what is considered the norm. We live in a world that tells us that when we lose someone, our pain is not palatable. We are expected to grieve quickly and quietly—to edit it out, lock it away, mask it, and move on—a message that only adds shame, self-judgment, and loneliness to so many other layers of heartache. This book is my father's brave attempt to give voice to the silence that is keeping so many of us isolated in our journey through loss.

This book is, in many ways, a love letter—not only to my mother but to the life they built together and the ache that remains in her absence. It is a plea to those whose lives have not been shattered by loss, asking them to do more now, while they still have time. What you'll find in these pages is honesty without editing. You will see a man walking through his life, his love, and his loss openly and without armor. My father has chosen not to turn away from or hide his sorrow; he walks into it and through it, offering his raw heart as a guide for anyone who dares to witness it. His thoughts and reflections are deeply human—tender, real, and always reaching toward finding meaning.

As a daughter, I read these words and see the man who loved and continues to love my mother deeply and without limits. I see a man who has grown and taken risks, living in ways that helps him to continue to feel connected to the woman that brought so much life into his.

As a therapist, I see courage in a man choosing to grieve out loud. I see strength in the honest expression of what so many people never feel brave enough to share with others. I see wisdom and hope shining through what often feels like the darkest of spaces.

This book is not just about loss. It's about all of it. It's about finding ways to carry not only the heaviness and the longing but also the joy, the memories, and the love. Losing the people we love can break us. But, if you dare to allow it, loss can also break us open. It can open us up to a deeper presence, deeper appreciation, deeper connections, and deeper love. If you dare to let it, it will open *you up to...*

Feel More

Care More

Laugh More

Live More

Love More

And Do More

. . . while you still have time.

May you find, in these pages, some solace in knowing that you are not alone. May you do more to live and love wholeheartedly and without pause. May you find, in my father's story, a companion of your own. May you allow yourself to let grief break you open to find the beauty and the magic that just might be there waiting for you underneath the pain.

—Rachel Kathleen Capurro, PsyD,
daughter and licensed clinical psychologist

Introduction

This solitary venture started in 2021 as an intimate personal journal, a chronological collection of thoughts and feelings, experiences and emotions, written down in those late-night moments when I was inspired to do so. My hope was that it would help me to cope with my feelings of pain and sorrow triggered by the loss of my wife of forty years.

The initial plan was that when I was no longer getting an emotional benefit from this expressive endeavor, I would stow a copy of it away somewhere in my home. Then at some point in time, after I had joined her on the other side, my daughters would find it, read it, and perhaps discover something of interest, something helpful, something inspiring. Maybe even something unknown about the relationship that I shared with their mother, the woman I have loved so deeply, for so very long. After that, if they felt it could be helpful, they could pass it on to others. But somewhere along the line this turned into something different, maybe something More.

The objective here, as it relates to this quest for spiritual and emotional healing, is to convey to you some of my thoughts regarding the experiences and life lessons acquired during the journey shared with my deceased wife, from the genesis of our relationship through the time beyond her passing. I believe, because of what I have been through and what I continue to experience, that I have something worth sharing. I would like to pass along some of what I have experienced and what I have felt, in a way that will allow you to have a better understanding as to how difficult it is to look back at the history of your loving relationships and realize that there were many missed opportunities to Do More to communicate the depth of the loving feelings you have for those special loved ones in your life.

The thoughts and suggestions shared here are inspired by her. They are intended to be a reminder to you to Do More for those you love, especially the one you love the most.

What I am sharing here is common sense stuff. In many instances, I am just stating the obvious. There is little in here that thoughtful, loving people do not already know. As you read this, you may think, "I already know this stuff." Which may be true. But this is not about what you know. This is about putting into practice what you know and applying it to your loving relationships. The truth is that the vast majority of us don't Do More often enough, even though we know we should. This is about utilizing the lessons learned throughout your life to be better at communicating your deepest feelings of love.

I would also like for you to get a glimpse, from my perspective, of what I believe to be a more realistic depiction of what it feels like to lose the one person who matters most to you. I'm attempting to paint a picture here, one that exposes the true reality of grief. My personal encounter with grief has caused me to recognize that the grief experience is not the journey that we have been led to believe it is, nor what we have perceived it to be.

If you're looking to discover a narrative here that is composed of intricate words and sophisticated ideas that will revive your loving relationships, you've probably come to the wrong place. But I believe that if you're looking to find some thoughts and reminders that come from the heart, that offer a bit of insight and some measure of inspiration, you may discover something here that will help you to be better in your loving relationships.

Please know that it is not my intention to bring you down or to make you sad or for you to feel pity for me, but rather to simply encourage you to Do More in your loving relationships and to remind you that love is what matters most.

While there is much included here that is a tribute to her, please understand that our story, my wife's and mine, is just a platform to get you thinking about your loving relationships, your story. As you read this, take your time, think about and reflect on the thoughts, experiences, reminders, and suggestions put forth in each paragraph. Think about what I have experienced in my relationship with her over the past several years and then picture yourself in my situation. Think of the situations presented here as if they were your own, as if they happened to you. Think about how losing the one person who matters most to you would impact your life. Most importantly, think about how you would feel emotionally after having experienced that level of loss.

Please understand that I would never, ever, in any way suggest that you or others have not experienced the type or the level of loss that I have or that my loss is more difficult or more painful than that of yours or others. I would never do that. We all know that a countless number of people die each day leaving loved ones behind to grieve. Loved ones that are absolutely devastated by the soul-searing pain from the loss of someone that they love so very deeply. Because of what I have experienced as a result of her passing, I now have deeper feelings of empathy, sadness, and love for those who have experienced the heartbreaking, life-altering pain that results from losing a special loved one.

Please know that as sad as I am from the loss that I have experienced, I cannot begin to imagine the pain of those who have lost a child or grandchild. Losing an adult whom you love is devastating, heartbreaking, but losing a child or grandchild, I cannot comprehend that level of loss. I do not have any understanding of that pain or how a person who experiences that type of loss ever comes back from that loss. My heart bleeds for those who have experienced the pain that comes from the loss of a child or grandchild.

Please do not interpret this to be me suggesting, in any way, that the thoughts, experiences, and reminders that I put forth here are easy to put into practice. As if, by reading this and then following through with it like it was some sort of relationship game plan, that you will then achieve a perfect loving relationship with the ones you love the most. Recognize that one of life's true realities is that matters of the heart are complex, they require much time, effort, and attention. The truth is that regardless of how much you accomplish in your loving relationships, there is always more that can be done. The goal is to be better, to do your best. This is all about improvement in our loving relationships. It's not about doing everything. It's just about Doing More.

It is my hope that on occasion this causes you to smile, that every now and then it brings you to tears, and, most importantly, that it continually gets you thinking.

Her name is Colleen. She is simply the greatest blessing of my life. To me, she was, is, and will always be the most emotionally and physically beautiful person in my life. Throughout her life, Colleen was intelligent, attractive, energetic, caring, open, honest, and healthy. That was the case until November of 2012, which is when she began experiencing serious health issues. At that time, her body was severely compromised by the development of debilitating allergic reactions, caused by the ingestion of or interaction with virtually all foods and scents. We were told that her illness affected two in a million people. She courageously battled her illness until March 10, 2021, which is when she passed on to what I am hopeful is a better place. She is the inspiration behind all that I do now, including this very personal composition.

In the early days of our relationship, I did not recognize what I had stumbled upon. That through fate, and despite my ignorance and immaturity, I was granted the opportunity to journey through life with a woman who was such a brilliant diamond. Who, over time, grew more spectacular, more beautiful.

Photo by Victor Anderson

I am not exactly sure when our story began because it started for her before it started for me. Let's just say that it wasn't a classic story of love at first sight. Although she was truly beautiful in so many ways, her external, physical beauty was not what initially attracted me to her. I recall her being there, being around, but not in a glorious, magical, breathtaking way. She was there, that person, that girl, who was so enormously full of energy, always looking for ways to have fun. Always looking to get into some sort of harmless mischief. She was a bit of a tomboy and quite the athlete. When it came to her group of friends, she was the straw that stirred the drink, she lit the fire. I must admit that there was a high level of attractiveness that came from the never-ending energy that she exuded. In the beginning she pursued me. Yet initially, I did not see her in the same light as she saw me. She was persistent in a friendly, relatively innocent, playful, subtlety flirtatious way. But at first, at least for me, it was not romance, it was fun, it was friendship.

Though I will say that she pursued me, make no mistake, she was not sitting around waiting for me. She was out having fun, interacting with her friends and with other guys. She was very strong-willed and was not going to put up with someone who would not commit to her. She was straightforward in her thinking, and she was clear and direct in how she expressed her thoughts and feelings, which will come as no surprise to anyone who ever knew her. She made it clear to me how she felt about me. She also made it crystal clear that she believed that I was afraid of commitment and that I was going to miss out on a very special, very beautiful, very personal loving relationship. I remember her sending me a note, telling me in her not-so-subtle way that I was blowing it, that I was a fool to not recognize that the feelings that we shared were much more than those of a simple friendship.

This beginning period of our relationship started around the fall of 1975, which was my senior year, her junior year of high school, and continued through the fall of 1976. In the late fall of 1976, I distinctly remember her calling me at my parents' home to tell me, in no uncertain terms, that she had had enough. She explained that she had very strong feelings for me, but that she felt, because of my unwillingness to commit to her, we would never have the loving relationship that she was looking for. She told me flat out that it was time for her to move on. She was so right to confront me and to essentially draw a line in the sand regarding our relationship. To this day I am so very thankful that she did. When directly and aggressively confronted with the reality of losing her, I realized just how much I cared for her, and I knew that I did not want to lose her. After a very long, passionate, and at times, heated conversation, which was essentially her chewing my ass for being self-centered, unkind, unappreciative, and unloving, and a lot of groveling and apologizing on my part, she agreed to give our relationship another chance. After that conversation, in which she completely and unapologetically kicked my ass, which I absolutely deserved, our loving relationship, through good times and hard times, continued until the day she passed. That conversation was simply the most important wakeup call of my life. I have loved her every day since. From that beginning, down the road of life we traveled. Living, learning, loving, doing our best, and like most everyone else, not Doing More often enough.

Love's Genesis

At the beginning just you and me,
Young and innocent, wild and free.
Hypnotized, and mesmerized, and captured,
Such indescribable, magical rapture.
Hearts filled with love's fire,
Bodies burning with youth's desire.
Both aspiring to discover,
Every detail of the other.
Every dream and every thought,
And every lesson we'd been taught.
Feelings not felt before or since,
A time of such beautiful, emotional innocence.

Before I get too deep into this, I must address something here or else the writing of this may appear to be me nominating Colleen for sainthood. I will tell you this; she was, without a doubt, no saint and no one knows that better than me. She was tough, she was strong minded, she was hardheaded, she was sassy, to the point of being a bit of a smart ass, actually, quite a bit of a smart ass. She was exceptionally intelligent, which on its own is a very good thing. The issue lay in the fact that she knew that she was much smarter than me, and she knew that I knew that she was much smarter than me and in a bit of a demented, mischievous way, the thought of that made her smile. To this day, I am certain that on many occasions she got great joy from being a gigantic pain in the ass to me and I loved her despite of it. Hell, truth be told, I may have, to some degree, loved her because of it.

Shortly after Colleen became ill in November of 2012, I realized that it was much more likely that she would die before I would, and sadly, so much younger than she should. Often, when I was alone, I would think about how life would be without her and how it would impact our daughters, our son-in-law, our family, our friends, and me. I knew that it would be a brutally difficult, heartbreaking experience. Over time, I thought that I had gained a reasonable understanding of what it would be like to lose her. I believed that I would be able to slowly navigate my way through the pain and would move forward. The problem with my thought process, as it related to losing the one person that I loved the most, is that I was assessing that deeply sad encounter with grief from the perspective of someone with no comparable experience, no true point of reference. The reality is that I had no idea of the magnitude of the grief that I would feel. I thought that I was at least somewhat prepared to be able to handle it. I was wrong. I was nowhere close to understanding how heartbreaking it would be. Losing someone that I have loved so deeply, over the entirety of my adult life, was just not comprehendible until I had lived through it. I now realize that I did not fully comprehend the true depth of our love, nor did I fully understand the sense of comfort and the level of dependence that came from having her in my life for all those years. There are no words that I can express or feelings that I can share that can fully prepare you for this experience. This type of loss is one of those life experiences that you must live through in order to gain a full understanding of that reality. You build your life around this special person, it is wonderful, not easy, not perfect, then one day they are gone. Your life will never be the same. You will never be the same.

Until They Go

I just don't know, that you'll ever know,
just how much you need them,
until they go.
I just don't know, that you'll ever know,
just how much you'll miss them,
until they go.
I just don't know, that you'll ever know,
just how much you love them,
until they go.

So, what do I mean when I say, Do More? Doing More is about making an ongoing, conscious effort to be better at demonstrating and communicating all the pieces that go into creating a deeper loving relationship.

Doing More is about being kinder. More caring. More open. More honest. More vulnerable. More emotional. More thoughtful. More encouraging. More comforting. More supportive. More loving. Doing More is doing all that it takes to fully demonstrate, communicate, express, and reinforce the feelings of love that you have for another person.

Throughout this when I speak of loss, I am not simply addressing the type of loss that comes about solely as a result of death but also the many life experiences that occur, that result in the deepest, most painful, heartbreaking feelings of sadness.

The message here is about Doing More for the ones you love the most, but here's the hard part about Doing More. While you are trying to focus on Doing More in your loving relationships, you must also do all the other typical life-related stuff too. You must work hard, raise your children, and interact with family and friends. You must address your adult responsibilities. You must deal with all of life's challenges, all of life's distractions. The reality is that being successful at Doing More is so much more complicated than just Doing More.

If I share my grief experience with you, and as a result you are motivated to Do More for the ones you love the most, isn't that a good outcome? As opposed to me keeping all my feelings of grief locked away, down deep inside and, as a result, no one learns from that experience.

When you initially fall in love, with your entire loving relationship ahead of you, when it comes to your hopes, dreams, and aspirations regarding how you envision your life together playing out, you certainly don't imagine it playing out in a scenario similar to how Colleen and mine has. I know the reality of my situation, but when it plays out like this, it's hard to believe and it's brutally difficult to accept. It's not that I don't believe that it could happen to me, but rather, I just don't accept that it could ever happen to her. She personified living. So energetic, so alive. To think of her as gone, is unthinkable, it's unacceptable to me. Though illogical, I still have this disbelief that she is gone.

I miss everything about her. Her beauty, her personality, her physical characteristics, her will to live, her intellect, her courage, her soft side, her sense of humor, her toughness, her spiciness, how much she cared, how much she loved, how much she sacrificed, how hard she fought to live. A never-ending stream of thoughts of her runs through my mind. We had so much more to do together. Live, laugh, talk, cry, plan, agree, disagree, share, spoil, love. This type of loss is a brutal reminder that every day is so very precious. That dreaded call, that devastating message, that unexpected knock on the door can happen to any of us, at any time.

Gone

Awaken to, sounds of breathing, hear her.
Slide on over, toward her, near her.
Her beside me, dozing there.
Smiling, dreaming, not a care.
Waking, yawning, stirring, stretching.
Moving, tempting, luring, fetching.
Her scent lingers in the air.
I reach for her but she's not there.

From that person that she fell in love with (the one influenced by the innocence and the freedom of youth), I evolved into that person that she needed me to be (the one influenced by the boundaries and responsibilities of adulthood). Sadly, I was not diverse enough to show a bit More of both sides of me More often, even though I tried. I am certain that at times she missed the youthful side of me. It's not that she didn't love me, she just would have liked to have experienced More of both sides of me. I get that. I wanted to share More of both sides of me for her as well. I too wanted More of both sides of her for myself. So do all you can to share both sides of you. Depending on the moment, depending on the situation, be diverse enough to share More of both sides of you More often.

12/30/2021

Tomorrow night marks the end of 2021. The saddest, most painful year of my life. I now face a future without the love of my life, my best friend, my true partner in life. Much of what we envisioned and planned for was focused on getting to this point in life. I now recognize something that I should have known many years ago. I should have been more focused on expressing my deep feelings of love for her, on appreciating everything beautiful about her, on living in the moment with her and less time spent worrying and planning for the years and the times that were yet to come, that ultimately, for her and me, will never come to be.

As time passes there is this inherent feeling of pressure for me to be okay, for me to fall in line with the grieving status quo. Which is saying that you're okay when clearly you are not. Which is burying your feelings of grief down deep inside. Which is never sharing your thoughts or your emotions related to your loss with those who love you. Which is not allowing yourself to be open, honest, and vulnerable. I get a sense that some people feel that I should stop being so naïve. That I should just bury my feelings of grief along with the feelings of love that I have for her. That I should keep it to myself and just move on. What if we were to break away from the grieving status quo? Stop keeping feelings of grief buried down deep inside. Stop pretending to be okay just because some people think that by now you should be okay. How about you admit that you're not okay? When it comes to living through grief, how about being honest with yourself and with others?

There is a societal norm that promotes a misleading perception as to how we are expected to deal with grief. I believe that many of those who have experienced the loss of a very special, very close loved one, attempt to work through their pain based on a perception of what they believe they had previously witnessed from others who were working through their grief experience. Typically, the view from the outside looking in appears to be a person that is working through the process of moving forward in a positive way. The truth is, that in many cases, they are suffering through the process. They are attempting to show the outside world that they are coping with the situation, that they are moving forward. In many cases, they are hiding or burying their true feelings and emotions. They put on a relatively happy face, but the truth is, they are not healing, they are suffering.

I believe that our personal grief experience should not be dealt with based upon misconceived societal norms but rather it should be addressed based upon the intimate, personal relationship that we shared with the one we've loved, the one we've lost. I believe that each person's grieving experience is as distinctive as the relationship that they shared with the person that they've lost.

As a result of her no longer being here with me, I have come to realize, now more than ever before, just how meaningful and beautiful the simple moments we shared together were, most of which were just part of our everyday life. Recognize that life has a way of distracting us from fully appreciating each other and from enjoying the beauty of those special moments that transpire when spent focusing on the ones we love. Don't allow the distractions of life to rob you of those precious times. Strive to recognize and to truly appreciate as many of those distinctive, precious moments as possible.

When it comes to the lack of understanding and the lack of perspective caused by the absence of communication regarding the deep, painful experience of grief caused by the loss of the one you love the most, the blame for that shortcoming should not be placed solely on those who have dealt with that experience. Some of the blame should also fall on those who have not yet had that experience. Given the right situation, wouldn't an open, honest conversation, initiated by the one who has not yet experienced that level of loss with the one who has, be beneficial to both?

We express our feelings of love with our words, through our actions, and by showing our emotions. In many instances, the expressions of our love tend to be subtle, somewhat understated. Certainly, that is okay, in fact, it is beautiful. But what if, every now and then, we took a deeper, more demonstrative approach to expressing our feelings of love? Instead of a simple I love you, what if, whether through our words, our actions, or our emotions, we express in detail why we love them, what we love about them, and how much we love them? Why not take advantage of those opportunities that present themselves to take a deep dive into our feelings of love and share them with the ones we love the most? The reality is that doing so is not something that is new to our deepest loving relationship. We did it when we first fell in love with our most special person. So, why not now?

At the beginning of a romantic, loving relationship there are not enough hours in the day. There is this unquenchable desire to discover everything about this unique, wonderful, beautiful, exciting person. There is just so much about them that's a mystery, an untapped wonderland of physical, intellectual and emotional characteristics just waiting to be unearthed and experienced. Sadly, at some point, the novelty begins to fade. Work, children, money, and adult responsibilities all impact our day-to-day life, which too often erodes our focus on the relationship. Understand and appreciate that love is the ultimate two-way street. It's a shared thing. A collective union. A partnership. It requires commitment and work from both partners to succeed, to flourish. Most importantly it requires communication. Through verbal and nonverbal communication, the partners share their thoughts, feelings, emotions, and desires. If you listen, if you focus, if you pay attention to the various lines of communication, the messages conveyed by your partner to you are there. It then falls upon you to recognize and to react, and then, in your own unique way, to communicate your thoughts, feelings, emotions, and desires to them.

When I speak of love as it relates to a romantic relationship, I mean for it to be inclusive of each of the many facets of love. Love is the emotional, intellectual, and spiritual connection shared by two people and it is also the raw, passionate desire for physical intimacy that burns in each of them.

Why is it, that as time passes, we recognize and appreciate the special blessings we have in our lives less and less, when in fact we should be appreciating those blessings more and more? Especially the blessing of love that we receive from those most special people in our lives.

So special and unique is the bond, the connection, the dependence that grows and evolves over the entirety of a long-term loving relationship. A relationship that will undoubtedly experience the ups and the downs, the thrills and the disappointments, the joy and the sorrow of a lifetime spent together. At some point in that long-term loving relationship there is, or there should be, this amazing, rewarding, beautiful realization that comes from knowing just how much love exists between the two of you.

Think of you and your lover/partner/spouse/friend in your long-term loving relationship. Now imagine that your situation becomes like my situation, where you have lost your most special person. Don't assume that it won't happen to you. Truth is, I assumed that nothing like that would ever happen to Colleen and me. As you imagine yourself having lost your greatest love, ask yourself, what could I have done to better demonstrate to the one I love the most, who I have now lost, how much I love her or him. The message here is simple; don't be waiting around to Do More. Do More now.

I believe that being successful in life and in love is about achieving balance among the various parts of our lives. Balance is achieved, to the best of our ability, by properly allocating our time and our mindset between work and home, responsibility and enjoyment. From what I have experienced and what I have observed of others, most of us struggle to find that balance. Sadly, for the most part, our society defines success or failure based on the amount of money and assets that can be amassed during our lifetime. As a result, many of us tend to focus too much of our time and effort into that pursuit. Because of that our personal relationships suffer. Money is not the only problem that tips the quest for balance in the wrong direction. The excesses of life's various vices such as drugs, alcohol, gambling, infidelity, and the quest for power and influence can all cause significant, destructive impacts upon our personal relationships.

Try to fully comprehend my reality, which at some point in time may become your reality. There are times when the longing that I feel for Colleen overwhelms me. When the emptiness saps my will. When the silence haunts me. When all I want in this world is her. Her, to see, to touch, to hear, to love. Think of all the wonderful, private, intense, emotional, exciting, fulfilling, touching, sensual, quiet, beautiful, loving moments that you now share with your lover. Then imagine that every bit of that is gone. Understand that you will never again see them, touch them, talk to them, share life's experiences with them. They are gone, completely and absolutely. There are no more shared smiles, laughter, tears, whispers, hugs.

Regardless of what others may think of the manner in which I deal with my feelings of grief, I know that it's okay to miss her, to be moved to tears, to not want to let go of the connection we have or of the love that we share.

Doing More is not about changing who you are. Rather, it's about being a better version of yourself, particularly as it relates to the relationship you share with those you love the most. It's about being more in the moment, more focused, more caring, more cognizant, and better at recognizing and acting upon opportunities to express the love that you feel for those special loved ones in your life.

In my mind, I often travel back to the many unforgettable experiences shared with her. Those memories can transport me back in time, to not only the visual perspective of the special occurrences, but also, to some measure, to the emotional ambiance that the events originally caused me to feel down deep inside. Through all the years, when we were both here together, there was a special connection to the beautiful memories of the past and an excited anticipation for the special times that were yet to come. Now that she is gone, there is this heartbreaking realization that there will be no new memories that directly include her.

When it comes to grief and the society that we live in, there seems to be this, "I'll soldier on alone" mentality. Why? Why is it that we shy away from sharing our grief experience with those closest to us? Why do we not discuss our journey through grief? Does the journey through grief have to be such a solitary experience? Wouldn't sharing the experience with certain people that we love and trust, who are open to the experience and want to help, be a positive experience for both the person that is grieving and the person that is wanting to help?

I believe that the "time heals all wounds" theory, when it comes to grief, is impulsively accepted by our society. This is probably the case because it allows people to believe that when they inevitably suffer a deeply painful loss that they will be okay as time passes. I see this as something that they need to believe because the alternative, that grief may not heal over time, is just too difficult to accept.

Early on in our relationship, when she and I were first falling in love, we experienced an enchanting, surreal, dreamlike connection. It felt as if she drew me into herself, allowing me to intimately, intellectually, and emotionally experience who she was. For those of you who are at the genesis of your loving relationship, as you are experiencing that initial magical period of falling in love, do not be in a rush to move on to the next phase of that loving relationship. The reality is that there is nothing as special, as unique, as beautiful as the feeling of falling in love. Allow yourself to enjoy everything about it for as long as you possibly can. You will never feel anything like it again.

Throughout this collection of prose and poetry, I endeavor to find the perfect words to portray the feeling of being in love. But the feeling of being in love is too special, too unique, too beautiful to be described by words alone. No collection of words, however combined, can come close to adequately conveying the feeling of a passionate kiss, a warm embrace, the feeling of attraction or of desire, nor the dreamlike feeling that overwhelms you when you are first falling in love. I think that being in love is comprised of an infinite assortment of indescribably magical feelings that are unique to each and every person who experiences love.

Over the entirety of our loving relationship, I felt her spirit, her passion, her energy, her emotion, her love. I was captivated by her beauty. I so deeply loved her. But, if I am honest, I must admit that I did not always communicate the full depth of my feelings for her to her, certainly not to the degree that I could have. The loss of her has caused me to think deeply about the totality and the pure beauty of her essence and of her presence. I now deeply regret that I was not better at expressing my deepest feelings to her related to how exceptionally distinctive and beautiful she was and how deeply I loved her.

I believe that most people would acknowledge that to truly live, we need love. So, after we find love, after we fall in love, why do we, over time, allow our expressions of the love we feel to become less and less of a priority? Why do we not savor every moment that we are in it and everything about it? Why do we not strive to express our deepest feelings of love to the one that we are so passionately in love with? Why do we allow something that is so extraordinary to become relatively ordinary? Because we allow life to get in the way, our loving relationships, which start out with so much potential, excitement, and beauty, too often stagnate, never attaining the near limitless upside that comes from love's magical journey.

Understand that money and material possessions play a significant role in life, including our loving relationships. Regardless of where money falls in the hierarchy of your loving relationships recognize that its impact is significant. Not enough or plenty, either way, money impacts our lives and our relationships. No two people agree on how much you need, how it should be shared, how it should be spent, how it should be saved. With money, like most things in a relationship situation, it's about communication and honesty. Do not minimize or downplay the impact of money. Ultimately, it's a complicated piece of the relationship puzzle.

The memories that I have of us are beautiful. Those memories take me back to special times in my life with her. The memories come to me continually, in times of reflection, through images in my mind, and from old familiar places that I see now. The hearing of certain verses of certain songs takes me back in time. The memories cause me to have flashbacks which trigger a desire to, once again, experience the feelings and emotions of falling in love and of sharing my life with her. Remembering those feelings and emotions can be a wonderful experience. Even recalling bits and pieces of those experiences can be so very special. The challenge to you is to recall and carry forward some of the memories and magical feelings and emotions that you experienced throughout your relationship with the one you love the most and then to allow those feelings and emotions to have a meaningful influence upon that loving relationship today.

Just a thought about being in love . . . when you are in it, you get to revel in the vastest array of emotional, spiritual and physical feelings and, if you are lucky, you get to experience it with your most special, once-in-a-lifetime person, and hopefully you get to enjoy that loving relationship over a very, very long period of time.

Each night I lay in bed, our bed, experiencing the same silence, the same longing, the same emptiness. Most nights now, as I am drifting off to sleep, I still whisper "Good night Colli. I love you." Then I wait patiently to hear her reply . . . Always waiting. Foolishly hoping. That's love.

Now and then I think back and remember some of the distinctive details of her physical makeup. The pure beauty of her hazel eyes, her soft supple skin, her inviting lips, her funny little feet. Her various hair styles, which were always in a constant state of change. Her perfect freckles, which in her younger years she felt such disdain for. Each of those many features were uniquely hers, genetically blended, resulting in my most beautiful girl. It's so very important in our loving relationships that over time we continue to recognize and appreciate the unique and beautiful characteristics of the one we love the most and that we take the time to communicate to them how absolutely beautiful they are to us.

When I think of a memory from our relationship, too often I remember it as a simple singular happening. I struggle to remember all the details that lead up to and that ultimately resulted in the creation of the memory. I understand that a memory is created based on a compilation of collective moments, of many details, of multiple contributing events and circumstances. I believe that it would be so fascinating in so many ways to be able to remember more of the moments, more of the small details of how certain memories came to be a memory. I'll give you one to think about. The first kiss that you shared with your most special person. For that moment, for that memory to be special it needs to be more than just the kiss. The memory needs to include the events, the moments, the many connected happenings that occurred prior to, that ultimately culminated in the memorable event, the kiss.

As time passes, it becomes more and more obvious that the days and the times of our youth were clouded by our many misjudgments and incorrect perceptions about life and about growing older. When we were young adults, we witnessed those elder to us and we assumed, we believed, that the fire of love, of passion, and of desire that burned deep within us would flicker and fade over time. Although there is a maturing over time of our love, our passion, and our desire, in those relationships where true love exists, the wonderful reality is that as time passes, that fire that we feel for our most special person continues to blaze down deep inside us.

When it comes to Doing More, recognize that you can overdo it. You need to be realistic. You need to be yourself. Communicating your feelings of love to someone special is not part of a rehearsed or premeditated plan. Doing More does not mean putting on some big production or creating some sort of drama to demonstrate your love. It's paramount that the communication of your love is genuine, heartfelt, and most importantly, personal. Personal in the sense that it's based on the reality of the life and the circumstances that the two of you share. Doing More is an in-the-moment endeavor. It needs to be a true expression, an honest display of the love you feel.

I notice that when I am in a group setting, whether it be out in public, at work, with a group of friends or family members, and I am asked how I am doing, I usually go into the mode of, "I'm okay." For the most part, when I'm in a group setting, I conceal much about my actual feelings and emotions. I essentially tell them what they want or need to hear. I don't want to get into my deepest feelings in a setting that I don't control. I find that I don't want to share where I'm at emotionally unless it's under my terms. I only want to share those very personal feelings and emotions with those people that care deeply about me and that honestly want to hear about my feelings of love, of loneliness, of heartbreak, of joy, and of sadness, and I only want to do that in a private, personal setting.

After Colleen passed, I had a personal encounter which, as it relates to grief, augmented my belief that many people hear what they want or need to hear. I crossed paths with someone that I knew from years ago. Early on in our conversation, this person, who knew of Colleen's passing, asked me how I was doing. Instead of going into my standard "I'm okay" response, I said that I wasn't great, that I was just hanging in there. The conversation went on to other subjects. At the end of our conversation, as we were parting, this person commented that it was good to hear that I was doing so well.

I have read and I have heard about others who have experienced the loss of their spouse, their partner, their special loved one, where they say, as it pertains to their loving relationship, that they have no regrets. I think that that is such bullshit. I do not get it. To say that you have no regrets is to say that you were perfect in that loving relationship. No way, no how. Only a fool would think that. The truth is, I did my best, but still I regret that I was not better at communicating to her how truly beautiful she was and how deeply I loved her.

I find that we work so hard at achieving success, as defined by our accumulation of monetary wealth, that we often fail at achieving success, as defined by our accumulation of beautiful experiences involving friendship and love.

For those who have been in a loving relationship for quite some time, remember back to the early years of that relationship when you and your spouse/partner/lover/friend went out on a date, to a party, to a movie, to dinner. Back then those outings were, for each of you, all about who you were with; that most special person in your life. The focus for each of you was on the other and on the loving relationship that the two of you shared. It was not about anyone or anything else. It was simply about being with your most special person, enjoying life with the one you love. Now, years later, why isn't that still the case?

One Wish

All that I wish for today,
and every day,
is all that I cannot have . . .
Her.

When you fall in love and that love survives the test of time, what you have achieved together is one of life's most meaningful, most beautiful accomplishments.

I understand that many of my friends and family members are uncomfortable talking to me about Colleen and the journey that we shared together. I believe that they think that if they mention her name in conversation that that will make me sad. The reality is that I am sad and it's not because someone asks me about her or about my life with her or about the pain I feel because she's gone. When someone has the opportunity to mention her in conversation, yet chooses not to, that makes me sad. Hearing someone talk about her in a loving, caring fashion helps me heal. It triggers my emotions. It makes me smile, it makes me laugh, it brings me back to her. And yes, it often makes me cry. And that's okay, because those tears come from my feelings of love for her. When someone has the courage to talk to me about her, it is a beautiful expression of their feelings of love for me and, more importantly, their feelings of love for her.

For me to say that I "miss" her is such an unconscionably ridiculous understatement. There's absolutely no correlation between a temporary absence and an every minute, every hour, every day, every month, every year disengagement. The first comes with a sense of anticipation, while the latter results in a never-ending state of sadness. Knowing that I will never see her, talk to her, touch her, share my experiences with her again in this time and place is indescribably painful. There is this constant, never-ending feeling of emotional numbness caused by her absence.

We all know that there is no going back in time, but there is or there should be lessons learned from the past which we should be applying to situations and decisions that occur in the present. It's important that we learn to enjoy the special times of our life by focusing on and appreciating the here and now. Learn from the past and make the effort to be better at enjoying what is happening right now, right there in front of you. Do not be constantly looking past today thinking that future events will be better than today. The reality is that tomorrow may never come. Live in the present, in the moment. Be more conscientious of the opportunities that life presents to you that you can use to positively impact your loving relationships today.

The Reality of Now

Now
the love I feel
is as all encompassing
as it was, when I was
first falling for her.
Now
I realize that
you can never, ever
get enough of
true love.
Now
the thoughts I have
of all the time spent
and all the love shared
are part magic and part despair.
Now
memories of her
make me smile
even in those moments
when tears spill from my eyes.

The loss of Colleen has changed me. It has, to a significant degree, broken me. But it has also gotten me to a place where I am much more focused on what is important in life. I now recognize, more than ever before, that there is just so much nonsense, so much drama, so much silly, selfish bullshit going on in our world. It appears to me that we have lost our moral compass and that we're losing our ability, and maybe even our desire to make our own way, to define our own life. When you feel the way that I do about life after losing her, you begin to truly recognize what really matters most in life.

The reality of life (and death) is that you get what you get. Throughout my adult life, I believed that I would have Colleen to love, to lean on, to share life's special moments with, at least into our 80's. But sadly, that has not happened. At times life can be, and should be, so much more than ordinary, more beautiful, more meaningful, more touching, more heartfelt, than you ever imagined it could be. But at times, life can be heartbreaking, soul-searing, and devastating.

I don't want you to perceive that Doing More is predominantly a quantitative pursuit, but rather one that is focused on achieving the highest qualitative effect. Yes, of course, more love is good; but deeper, truer, more meaningful, more honest, more open love results in a much more desirable, beautiful loving relationship.

Over the course of our deepest loving relationship most of us took the time to write a letter, a note, a poem, or a card where we were open, honest, and vulnerable. We shared our deepest feelings of love with our most special person. How long has it been since you did something like that? Probably too long. What are you waiting for?

Many of my friends and family members perceive that I am okay, that I am moving forward in a positive way. Please know that although you may see me smile or hear me laugh, it doesn't mean that I am not sad or that I have let go of her or that I have moved on from the loving relationship that I have shared with her. It does not mean that I don't long to see her, to hold her, to love her. It just means that I am doing what I can to carry on. Please understand that I am carrying on even though there is much of me that is broken. Just because you don't see me cry, doesn't mean that it's not happening.

The obvious fact is that my life will never be the same. I cannot wish it or hope it back to what it once was with Colleen. I know that I need to focus on moving forward, but the truth is, that reality comes with many brutally difficult challenges. Just the simple process of arriving home from work each night is fraught with emotional distress. When I pull into the driveway, I know that I will soon be entering a house that is dark and silent. That silence perpetuates a growing feeling of emptiness, of loneliness. As I make my way through the house all I hear are the soles of my shoes lightly contacting the floor beneath me. Every room I enter is filled with memories and reminders of our life together. I can envision her here. I can see her smile. I can hear her laugh. I remember how truly beautiful she was. When I go to sleep each night, it is completely quiet. In those quiet moments I miss everything about her. I miss her stirring beside me. I miss the sound of her breathing. There are no sounds of her dreaming or of her talking in her sleep. Just silence. It's all a very real reminder that she's no longer here with me. So, treasure each and every moment of the journey shared with the ones you love the most. Understand that when they are no longer here, you will long for them deeply and in more ways than you could ever imagine.

There is an unspoken, beautifully deep, peaceful connection when lovers, partners, friends are comfortable just being together, sharing the silence, appreciating the view, enjoying the moment, experiencing love.

Illustration by Bob Koehler

In our society, we strive to have more. More money, more power, more influence, more success. I now understand that if I had achieved everything I believed, as a relatively young adult, that I wanted to achieve in terms of both personal and financial goals, I would still be here, in this same situation, in this same state of mind as I am now, simply wishing that I could trade what I have in exchange for having her here with me once again. To wake up with her each morning. So happy to be with her. Holding her close. Talking. Expressing to her, that without her in my life, my life could never be as special or as beautiful or as colorful as it is. To be with her each day, absolutely appreciating all that she is. Recognizing that she has been and always will be my #One. For all of you who still have your #One, are you fully appreciating them? Are you expressing and demonstrating the deep feelings of love that you have for them? Each morning, when the two of you wake up, recognize that life has given you that day together, to share with each other. Always remember that tomorrow is not a certainty for any of us. Enjoy, appreciate, and treasure each and every day spent with the one you love the most, because when those days are done, trust me, they are absolutely done.

On occasion think back and recall from your earliest days together, the focused effort you made to share and express your deepest feelings of love to the one you love the most. Remember how you felt physically and emotionally when you first fell in love. Why not strive to remember, to rekindle, to recapture even the smallest pieces of those magical falling-in-love moments. Then allow those feelings to impact your deepest loving relationship today.

Living life following the death of your most special person results in a deeply emotional, bittersweet existence between the painful sadness which you endure and the beautiful love that you continue to feel.

I have come to the realization that if you absolutely love someone, no matter how much you did during your time together to show your love, after they pass, you will always feel that you could have done more. As time has passed since Colleen's death, this feeling of not having done enough for her has consumed me. Though I did my best, still I regret not Doing More, more often. I know that none of us are perfect, that we will not always take advantage of the opportunities that are there for us to act on. Still, I know that making our absolute best effort to Do More for those we love the most is what we must strive to do.

The personal, spiritual, and emotional growth that I have experienced since she passed is such a bittersweet accomplishment. It has been uplifting, enlightening, touching, and so very beautiful. Yet, I am devastated and angry that I did not attain, I did not develop more of that meaningful, beautiful knowledge until after she had departed.

When the one you love the most dies, the love you feel, the love you have shared with them over the course of your relationship, does not go away. That love carries on in your heart, mind, and soul. That love survives and, in a way, it takes on something of a life of its own. The memories of your life with your loved one rattle around inside your head. They play out and are scrutinized by you repeatedly. Some of those memories make you smile; some make you cry. Some give you profound emotional pleasure; some leave you with deep feelings of regret.

If the pain and sadness of our grief exists because our feelings of love for our most special person continue to live on, would we choose to let the love we feel, that has been with us for so very long, diminish over time to free ourselves from the grief? I say hell no. I say we strive to live a life where we work at balancing the life that we once had, with our present life. Our present life, where we live in the moment and we celebrate the love that we feel in the here and now, while still retaining feelings of love, memories, and lessons learned from the past, from the ones we loved so deeply, for so very long.

It seems that somewhere along the line many people forget that love is the greatest, most beautiful gift in life. After having experienced the blessing of falling in love, of being in a beautiful, loving relationship, they seek something new, something that they believe is more important, more fulfilling, more exciting. They allow themselves to be enamored by, and believe that, things like money, power, possessions, and infidelity are more desirable than love. They toil in their quest to attain more. When they begin to recognize that more may not bring them fulfillment, excitement, or happiness they attempt to convince themselves that it does. But it doesn't. Over time they come to know that having more things doesn't measure up to love. Often, by the time that they come to that realization, the beautiful loving relationship that they had is gone.

While the loss of your most special person is unimaginably sad and painful, still there exists a feeling within you that is so emotionally and spiritually beautiful. That feeling comes from knowing that you have loved this wonderful person with all your heart and to the absolute depth of your soul.

Illustration by Bob Koehler

I am having a hard time believing in the theory that "time heals all wounds." I thought based on that theory, with the passing of each year, those most difficult occasions in life would become less painful. For example, on living through the specific day on which she passed or on her birthday or when we celebrate Christmas. Those events are not getting easier. With each passing year, it just feels like the space between she and I is growing larger, the nights longer, the pain deeper.

The obvious reality here is that I cannot force you to Do More in your loving relationships. I can only provide suggestions. I can only nudge you in that direction. Ultimately, it's up to you to decide if your loving relationships are worth making the effort it takes to Do More.

Tears

Always just a memory away.
Sometimes they trickle, sometimes they pour.
In most instances, you can feel them coming,
but occasionally, they sneak up on you.
Though they come from the pain,
the emotion and the heartbreak you feel,
at times they can help settle you,
bring you a sense of peace,
and, maybe, a bit of healing.

The view from where I am now is much clearer and the opportunities to Do More, that I often failed to recognize, now seem quite obvious. Sadly, this sense of clarity often escaped me in my younger days.

There are events in life that you hope you will never fully comprehend because the only way to fully comprehend the impact of the event is to experience the pain caused by the occurrence of the event firsthand. That is what occurs when you love someone to the depth of your soul and then you experience the heartbreaking pain of losing that once-in-a-lifetime person. My grandfather, John, lost his wife, Marie, in June of 1976. The depth of his love and the weight of losing her broke him. He was always a truly wonderful, special person. One that I still deeply love. But he was never the same after she passed. Until I lost Colleen, I never fully comprehended the pain that resulted from his loss, nor the depth of his love for her. Until now, I never fully understood what it meant to be broken.

The excuse we use far too frequently for not Doing More, more often, is that "life gets in the way." While it is often true that life does have a way of getting in the way of expressing the love we feel, the reality is, it doesn't always get in the way. There are many opportunities that become available to us to Do More. It falls on us to identify those opportunities and then to step up and take the initiative to act on them.

Often now the word "bittersweet" comes up in conversation as it relates to the memories I have and the times that I shared with Colleen. In many instances I've noticed that the word bittersweet gets used without sufficient context as to the breadth of the feelings that it encompasses. Understand that there is a vast emotional crevice between the painful, bitter lows of loss and grief, and the beautiful, sweet highs of friendship and love.

I believe that Doing More is contagious. I believe that those who receive More Love from you can't help but to reciprocate in a beautiful, loving manner.

How

So how in the hell do I ever move on,
When the woman I've loved, forever, is gone.
Those she loved, now we're grieving.
Not a one, accepts her leaving.
Each life touched, loved, and savored.
To so many, a true lifesaver.
Her mind so open and so honest.
Until her illness thrust upon us.
Not one to hold back on her thoughts.
With unmatched courage on she fought.
If there'd be an issue, she'd face it.
A difficult challenge, head on she'd embrace it.
Not one to allow her constant pain define.
Her life lived here on earth divine.
When you love one like her, then sadly
she is gone.
How in the hell can you ever expect
to move on?

Unfortunately, for most of us, it takes a significant portion of our lives to recognize, to come to the realization that our most special person is a once-in-a-lifetime blessing. Be thankful for and appreciative of that blessing. Do not squander the opportunity that life has given you to truly love that most special, beautiful person.

12/15/2023

Christmas time of year, home sitting, gazing at the Christmas tree, which my daughters, my son-in-law, my grandchildren, and I decorated. It looks so very beautiful, but something is not quite right, not quite perfect. In my mind's eye, I can envision how it looked when it felt perfect to me. It felt perfect to me when Colleen decorated it. I had always thought that it was perfect because of all the time that she put into placing each ornament, each strand of lights where they looked their very best. The reality is that it was perfect to us because she put so much love into making it just right, as she did with most every task she addressed. Through her actions, she communicated to us that she loved us and that nothing mattered more to her than us. So, there is a reason that the tree does not seem quite right, not quite perfect. It's her. And it's not because she isn't the one decorating the tree. Rather, it's because after the tree has been decorated, regardless of who does the placing of the lights and the ornaments, when all of that is finished and the tree is beautiful, it's not perfect now because she's not here to share the warmth, the beauty, the love together with all of us. While you still have your most special loved ones here, appreciate them, cherish them, because nothing is truly right, truly beautiful, truly perfect without them.

People say that the memories will get you through the grief. I have been truly blessed to have experienced forty-four years of making countless, beautiful memories with Colleen, but those memories do not take away my feelings of grief. The memories help in that they can be a distraction from the grief. For me now, the memories and the grief are two parts of my life that coexist in my mind. The memories take me back to so many beautiful times, places, and situations, including falling in love, building a relationship, a friendship, a life-long bond. The memories can distract you from the pain, from the sadness, from the loneliness, but only for a period of time. The memories cannot fix you. At times, the memories can result in the magnification of the pain, sadness, and loneliness. That is not to say that I would ever want the memories to be forgotten. The memories are truly wonderful. They are so vivid that they can visually and emotionally take me back to the time and place when the memory occurred. They can bring back those feelings of being together, having fun, being in love. The memories are so beautiful, but they do not take away my feelings of grief.

Celebrate those you love, every day, every time you see them, every time you speak to them, every time you part ways. Do not assume that you will see or hear from them again. There are no guarantees, so at each and every opportunity, show them, and tell them that you love them. And always take the time to enjoy, cherish, and appreciate the love that those who care deeply about you send your way. Never take that love for granted.

Though intellectually we know that we don't, we often act as if we have forever. Forever to live, to laugh, to appreciate, to share, to comfort, to love . . . How foolish of us.

Colleen took the time to appreciate the moments in life that many of us take for granted. When I see or experience something now, sights or happenings that in the past I may have taken for granted, I try to focus on them and fully appreciate them as she would. As a result, I am now seeing more of the specialness and the beauty of life. Even the smallest things make life better. Going forward, I will focus on enjoying those moments with my daughters, my son-in-law, my grandchildren, our families, and our special friends. I will share those moments with Colleen by keeping her in my heart and in my thoughts, and, in some fashion, present with me in those moments. Do yourself a favor, take the time to recognize and fully appreciate all that is special in the world around you.

Once you have lost that most special person in your life, there's nothing that you can do to make amends with them for the mistakes and missed opportunities that occurred when they were here with you. For those of you who have that most special person in your life, you still have time. So, be aware. Open your eyes, your mind, and your heart. The opportunities are there, right in front of you. Don't just sit there on your ass, they won't jump in your lap. Focus, recognize, and act on them. Do something unexpected in a very personal and beautiful way. Show that most special person, in ways big and small, just how much you love them.

I get it. Life can't be all fantasies and fairytales. It can't be love, love, love twenty-four hours a day, every day. As adults, we have certain responsibilities that must be fulfilled, that take up much of our time, that require our full attention. But certainly, there can be, within a responsibly lived life, More love.

Over the course of my adult life, there have been times when I was talking to or thinking of a person that I love, when a caring, complimentary, or beautiful thought about them entered my mind. But instead of sharing it with them, at times I would think, "well that goes without saying." As a result, in many instances, I may not have shared it with them. But now, given the experiences of the last several years of my life, when it comes to sharing a caring, complimentary, or beautiful thought about someone who I love, I recognize that nothing like that should ever go without saying.

The way that I cope with her passing may change as time goes on, but the love I feel for her will remain. I shall stay connected to her, grounded by all that I have learned from her. I will not move away from her emotionally, but I will, little by little, with love for her in my heart, take steps to move forward. This writing adventure has become a labor of love. It has aided me in my healing journey. It's allowed me to see myself in a drastically different light. It's helped me to be more open and honest with myself and with others. Regardless of where this process ultimately takes me, it has given me such a beautiful feeling of emotional satisfaction and a greater level of connection to her and to many others as well. I continue to feel love for her and from her, certainly a uniquely, beautifully altered version of the love that I experienced when she was alive, but still, one that touches me deeply.

At times, I get to thinking about how much Colleen suffered through both the physical and the emotional pain inflicted upon her by her illness and just how hard she fought to live. After she became ill, Colleen created a special wake-up message to motivate herself to keep fighting each day. That simple two-word message was "Just Stay." It was programmed into her phone to pop up each morning, "Just Stay." Do whatever it takes, "Just Stay." Fight like hell, "Just Stay." The physician side of her caused her to study and research her own illness hoping to find a cure that would allow her to, "Just Stay." And that is what she did, for 8½ years. During that time, though often in pain, she lived, laughed, and loved. She painstakingly planned and joyously danced at each of our daughter's weddings. With never-ending love in her heart and tears in her eyes, she was here to experience the births of each of our four beloved, beautiful grandchildren. There was something deeply touching and so very beautiful about the way that she lived and how hard she fought. Much of the emotional pain that she dealt with as she attempted to "Just Stay," occurred when she was alone with her thoughts and emotions. To protect those that she loved, she kept much of the pain, much of the emotional suffering, and the sadness to herself. Throughout her battle, she willed herself to be mentally and emotionally tough in order to "Just Stay." She fought an amazing battle out of love for those most special people in her life. For her it was this simple. Because she loved and was so deeply loved, she fought. For her there was no other reason to fight, except for love. Throughout her life, she cared more, she fought harder, she inspired many, she loved deeper. Throughout her life she did so much More than Just Stay.

Remembering Her

Whether out for a walk or out for a drive,
Remembering her, so beautiful and so alive.
Memories of her, oh so very dear,
From long ago, then tears appear.
Whether a trickle or a stream,
Can't wash away this very sad dream.

The emotional impact of her death has changed who I am and how I see myself. Now, I want to be kinder, more caring, more open, more honest, more empathetic, more loving. I have zero tolerance for selfishness, prejudice, hatred, greed. I have no interest in small talk. I am infinitely less tolerant of my many shortcomings. I want to surround myself with people who are kind, interesting, intelligent, unique, emotional, trustworthy, self-aware, open, honest, and loving. I want to discover pieces of her within me and in those that I love. I want to be more like her.

Do More for the one you love the most

in ways that are:

tender

touching

warm

sensual

kind

emotional

beautiful

vulnerable

passionate

pleasurable

private

personal

Even Though

Even though I can no longer hear her voice,
it doesn't mean she no longer speaks to me.

Even though I can no longer feel her touch,
it doesn't mean I am no longer touched by her.

Even though she no longer resides here
with me,
it doesn't mean she no longer lives down deep
inside me.

Even though she's no longer a star here
on Earth,
it doesn't mean she's no longer somewhere
twinkling!

When I think about it, I now realize that what I received from her was a special life-changing blessing and that what she did for my soul was pure beauty. Over the course of our life together, she changed me. She made me a different person, a better person. One that felt what it was like to love and to be loved. All that she did for me throughout the years, lives on within me. It gives me this comforting feeling of warmth, of love, but it also causes a never-ending feeling of longing for her.

There have been a few occasions where friends and family members have, out of love for me and in a very caring manner, hinted, or suggested that I begin moving forward in a positive emotional direction. I believe that those hints and suggestions were, in some way, prompted by her. In those instances, at least up to this point, I have pushed back to some degree by expressing to my friends and family, and to her, that I wanted to continue to remember us on our path together for just a bit longer.

I did not take our relationship for granted. I believe that she and I recognized that we shared a special bond. I suppose that it is natural to now think that I should have Done More for her when I had the opportunity. But I know that I truly loved her, and I am certain that she knew that I truly loved her and maybe that is enough, maybe that's as good as it gets.

For Eternity

clear cool water deep,
vast blue sky above,
here, back in the day,
we felt such joy and love.
you, there on the beach,
such a sight to see,
your natural beauty,
your spirit free.
beneath umbrellas,
where you'd lay,
with your thoughts,
at end of day.
the most captivating beauty,
of this heavenly place,
was seeing each day,
your gorgeous, smiling face.
I'd give so much,
selfishly on my behalf,
to hear once more,
your joyful, infectious laugh.

here, the beauty and the wonder,
of your spirit shared,
with all, in the many ways,
your soul was bared,
to hold and love,
and comfort you,
was the treasure,
i was blessed to do.
this was the vision,
that you forever saw,
this, your happy place,
this, your shangri-la.
a final voyage across,
this your favorite place,
to you and all of us,
a forever, sacred space.
one day again i'll find you,
here is where you'll be,
then it's us together,
here forever,
for eternity.

Sometimes now, on perfectly peaceful summer evenings, I will venture outside to my backyard to experience the beauty that only nature can offer. With thoughts of her in my mind, I'll gaze at the magnificence surrounding me illuminated by the light of a full moon. I'll hear the soothing sounds of soft breezes through branches of tall pines and of wind chimes whispering in my ears. I'll smell the fragrance of freshly mown grass. I'll feel the dampness, the coolness of the evening air. On occasion, the quiet of night will be disrupted by the muffled sound of a motorcycle's roar in the distance. In those moments, I am taken back in time to the small town that she and I grew up in. I recall the many evenings that she and I spent talking, planning, and laughing long into the night, our feelings of love for each other growing deeper. But time moves on. I know that when morning dawns, the sun will soon be shining upon a world that is different from the one that she and I knew. Now, the world that we knew and the life that we shared, no longer exist. And sadly, the opportunities for me to Do More for her, here on Earth, have passed.

Illustration by Bob Koehler

About the Author

Photography by AB Photography
Samantha Bearden, Owner

Brad Capurro prefers not to have a traditional author bio and itemize his academic and professional accomplishments, as they do not properly define who he is. What matters most—and best defines him—are the personal relationships he's had with those most special people in his life: his loving family and many wonderful friends. To Brad, each of those relationships is a true blessing, a unique and beautiful accomplishment.

www.ingramcontent.com/pod-product-compliance
Lightning Source LLC
Chambersburg PA
CBHW021824090726
47818CB00077BA/35

9781966981220